MANAGING NEGATIVE EMOTIONS FOR HIGHLY SENSITIVE WOMEN

How to Declutter Your Mind from Negativity, Deal with Stress, Resentment, and Anxiety, Calm Your Inner Critic and Embrace Emotional Strength

SANDY MATHIAS

TABLE OF CONTENTS

INTRODUCTION

As I sit down to write this book, I am reminded of a moment from my own life that sparked the journey toward understanding and managing negative emotions as a highly sensitive woman. It was a particularly challenging day at work, where the demands seemed insurmountable, and the environment felt overwhelming. Despite my best efforts to keep up, I found myself drowning in a sea of stress, anxiety, and self-doubt. In that moment, I realized that my sensitivity wasn't just a character trait; it was a fundamental aspect of who I was, shaping how I experienced the world around me and influencing my emotional landscape.

This realization led me on a quest to explore the intricacies of being a highly sensitive woman and to understand the unique challenges we face when it comes to managing negative emotions. Along the way, I encountered countless others who shared similar struggles – women who grappled with stress, resentment, anxiety, and the relentless voice of their inner critic. It became clear to me that there was a need for a resource that not only validated these experiences but also provided practical strategies for navigating them with grace and resilience.

In this book, I aim to fill that void by offering a comprehensive guide to managing negative emotions for highly sensitive women. Drawing from my personal experiences, as well as insights from psychology, neuroscience, and mindfulness practices, I will explore the complexities of our emotional landscape and provide actionable steps for decluttering the mind from negativity, cultivating inner peace, and embracing emotional strength.

Throughout these pages, I will share stories of triumph and setbacks, weaving together anecdotes from my own life with lessons learned from others who have walked similar paths. Together, we will delve into the science behind negative emotions, uncovering the underlying mechanisms that drive our thoughts, feelings, and behaviors. We will explore the power of emotional awareness, learning to identify and understand the myriad of emotions that course through our veins on a daily basis.

But this book is more than just a theoretical exploration of the human psyche. It is a practical guide filled with tools and techniques designed to empower you on your journey toward emotional well-being. From stress management strategies to techniques for quieting your inner critic, each chapter is packed with actionable advice that you can implement in your own life, starting today.

As we embark on this journey together, I invite you to approach these pages with an open mind and a compassionate heart. Know that you are not alone in your struggles, and that there is hope for a brighter, more emotionally resilient future. By embracing our sensitivity as a source of strength rather than a weakness, we can learn to navigate the ups and downs of life with grace and courage.

So, dear reader, I invite you to join me on this transformative journey toward emotional empowerment. Together, let us embark on a path of self-discovery, healing, and growth, as we learn to manage our negative emotions and embrace the fullness of who we are as highly sensitive women.

CHAPTER 1

UNDERSTANDING HIGHLY SENSITIVE WOMEN

IMPORTANCE OF MANAGING NEGATIVE EMOTIONS FOR HIGHLY SENSITIVE WOMEN

Emotions are an inherent aspect of human experience, influencing our thoughts, behaviors, and relationships. While experiencing a range of emotions is normal and healthy, the ability to manage negative emotions is crucial for overall well-being. This holds especially true for highly sensitive individuals, particularly women, who often navigate a world that can be overwhelming due to their heightened emotional sensitivity.

Emotional sensitivity refers to an individual's heightened responsiveness to emotional stimuli from both internal and external sources. Highly sensitive individuals tend to process sensory information deeply, leading to intense emotional reactions to stimuli that others may not even notice. While emotional sensitivity is not exclusive to any gender, research suggests that women, on average, tend to score higher on measures of emotional sensitivity compared to men (Aron et al., 2010). This heightened sensitivity can be attributed to a combination of biological, psychological, and societal factors.

For highly sensitive women, negative emotions can manifest in unique ways compared to individuals with lower sensitivity levels. HSWs may experience more intense emotional responses to stimuli such as criticism, conflict, or overwhelming environments. Due to their heightened empathy and awareness of subtle cues, HSWs may also be more susceptible to absorbing the emotions of others, leading to emotional overwhelm or burnout. Moreover, HSWs may struggle with regulating their emotions, finding it challenging to bounce back from setbacks or distressing situations.

The consequences of unmanaged negative emotions for HSWs can be significant and far-reaching. Persistent feelings of stress, anxiety, or sadness can take a toll on both physical and mental health, increasing the risk of conditions such as depression, chronic pain, and autoimmune disorders (Pluess & Belsky, 2013). Unmanaged negative emotions can also strain relationships, as HSWs may struggle to express their needs effectively or set boundaries to protect their emotional well-being. Additionally, the cumulative effect of suppressing or ignoring negative emotions can lead to emotional numbness or detachment, further exacerbating feelings of isolation or disconnection.

CHARACTERISTICS OF HIGHLY SENSITIVE WOMEN

Highly sensitive women embody a unique blend of traits and characteristics that profoundly influence their experiences and interactions with the world. At the core of their being lies a heightened sensitivity to various stimuli, encompassing emotions, sensory input, and environmental factors. This sensitivity manifests in the depth of their processing, as they tend to analyze and reflect on experiences with remarkable detail and complexity. For highly sensitive women, a simple conversation or interaction can evoke a plethora of thoughts and emotions, as they delve deep into the nuances of tone, body language, and underlying feelings. This propensity for introspection and reflection enriches their understanding of themselves and others, fostering deeper connections and insights.

Moreover, highly sensitive women often find themselves easily overwhelmed by external stimuli, such as noise, crowds, and bright lights. This overstimulation sensitivity can lead to feelings of anxiety or exhaustion in stimulating environments, prompting the need for solitude and calm to recalibrate and recharge. Highly sensitive women may seek refuge in quiet spaces or natural settings, where they can find solace amidst the chaos of the world. Their ability to recognize and honor their need for self-care is essential for maintaining emotional balance and well-being in a society that often values busyness and stimulation.

In addition to their sensitivity to external stimuli, highly sensitive women possess a deep emotional reactivity and empathy towards others. They experience emotions intensely and demonstrate a keen awareness of subtle emotional cues, making them adept at navigating complex interpersonal dynamics. Highly sensitive women often find themselves attuned to the emotional needs of those around them, offering support and comfort with compassion and understanding. Their innate ability to connect with others on a profound level fosters meaningful relationships built on trust, authenticity, and mutual respect.

Furthermore, highly sensitive women exhibit a sensitivity to subtleties in their environment, including nuances in social interactions, art, or music. They are attuned to the beauty and intricacies of the world, finding inspiration and solace in the simple joys of everyday life.

Highly sensitive women may possess a heightened appreciation for art, literature, or music, finding comfort and inspiration in creative expression. Their ability to find beauty and meaning in the mundane enriches their lives and allows them to experience profound moments of awe and wonder.

COMMON CHALLENGES THEY FACE

Highly sensitive women (HSWs) face a myriad of challenges stemming from their heightened sensitivity to various stimuli, which can significantly impact their well-being and quality of life. One of the most prevalent challenges is overwhelm, as HSWs may easily become overstimulated by loud noises, crowded spaces, or intense emotions. For instance, a busy shopping mall or a noisy party can quickly become overwhelming for an HSW, leading to feelings of anxiety and distress. Additionally, HSWs often contend with the intensity of their emotions, which can be both a blessing and a burden. While their depth of emotional experience enriches their lives, it also means that they may feel emotions more acutely, leading to heightened levels of stress or vulnerability.

External factors such as criticism or conflict can exacerbate these challenges for HSWs. Highly sensitive women are particularly sensitive to criticism, as they may internalize negative feedback and ruminate over it for extended periods. Even well-intentioned criticism can feel deeply personal and hurtful to an HSW, impacting their self-esteem and confidence. Similarly, conflicts or confrontations can be highly distressing for HSWs, who may struggle to cope with the emotional intensity of such situations. Their heightened empathy and sensitivity to social dynamics make it difficult for them to navigate interpersonal conflicts without feeling overwhelmed or emotionally drained.

The cumulative impact of these challenges can take a toll on the mental and physical health of HSWs. Chronic stress, anxiety, and emotional dysregulation are common among HSWs, as they navigate a world that often feels overwhelming and emotionally taxing. Moreover, the constant effort to manage their sensitivity and cope with external stressors can contribute to feelings of exhaustion and burnout. Physical health issues such as headaches, muscle tension, and gastrointestinal problems may also arise as a result of chronic stress and emotional dysregulation.

EMBRACING YOUR SENSITIVITY AS A STRENGTH

Sensitivity is often misunderstood and unfairly labeled as a weakness, yet it is a valuable asset that can enrich every aspect of life when embraced and nurtured. Highly sensitive women (HSWs) possess a unique set of qualities that empower them to navigate the world with depth, empathy, and creativity. Rather than viewing sensitivity as a burden, it's time to recognize it as a source of strength and resilience.

First and foremost, sensitivity is synonymous with empathy – the ability to understand and share the feelings of others. HSWs have an innate capacity to connect with people on a profound level, offering support, compassion, and understanding in times of need. This empathy fosters deeper, more meaningful relationships built on trust and mutual respect, enriching both their personal and professional lives.

Creativity is another hallmark of sensitivity, as HSWs possess a rich inner world brimming with imagination and insight. Their ability to perceive subtleties and nuances in their environment fuels their creativity, inspiring innovative solutions to complex problems and fresh perspectives on familiar concepts. Whether it's through art, music, writing, or problem-solving, HSWs have a unique gift for turning their sensitivity into something beautiful and transformative.

Deep thinking is a natural byproduct of sensitivity, as HSWs tend to process information deeply and reflect on experiences with great depth and complexity. This depth of processing allows them to uncover hidden truths, explore new ideas, and gain profound insights into themselves and the world around them. Rather than shying away from their introspective nature, HSWs can embrace it as a powerful tool for personal growth and self-discovery.

To leverage their sensitivity in their relationships, careers, and personal lives, HSWs can incorporate practical strategies into their daily routines. Cultivating mindfulness and self-awareness can help HSWs navigate their emotions more effectively, allowing them to recognize and regulate their responses to external stimuli. Setting boundaries and prioritizing self-care are essential practices for HSWs, enabling them to protect their energy and maintain emotional balance in a demanding world.

I offer a message of hope and empowerment to all highly sensitive women (HSWs) who may have felt misunderstood or undervalued in a world that often overlooks their unique qualities. Your sensitivity is not a weakness but a remarkable strength that sets you apart and empowers you to make a profound impact on the world around you. Embrace your empathy, creativity, and deep thinking as powerful tools for personal growth and positive change.

Remember that you are not alone on this journey. There is a community of highly sensitive individuals who understand and appreciate your sensitivity, offering support, validation, and encouragement along the way. Surround yourself with people who celebrate your uniqueness and uplift you in times of doubt or uncertainty.

Trust in your ability to navigate life with grace and authenticity, honoring your needs and staying true to yourself amidst the noise and chaos of the world. Your sensitivity is a gift that enables you to forge deeper connections, inspire creative solutions, and bring light to dark places.

As you embrace your sensitivity as a source of strength and resilience, may you find the courage to pursue your passions, fulfill your dreams, and live a life filled with purpose and meaning. You are capable of extraordinary things, and the world is waiting to be transformed by your unique perspective and contributions. So, stand tall, embrace your sensitivity, and let your light shine brightly for all to see. You are worthy, you are enough, and you have the power to thrive.

CHAPTER 2

UNRAVELING YOUR EMOTIONS

As a highly sensitive woman (HSW), understanding what triggers negativity, both internally and externally, is crucial for your emotional well-being and resilience.

Triggers are stimuli that elicit strong emotional responses, rooted in past experiences, beliefs, and thought patterns. As a highly sensitive woman, you possess a heightened sensitivity to stimuli and emotions, making triggers particularly impactful on your mental and emotional state.

Internal Triggers:

Internal triggers often originate from your thoughts, beliefs, and inner dialogue. These can include self-criticism, perfectionism, and feelings of inadequacy. For example, you may experience overwhelming self-doubt when faced with a challenging task, questioning your abilities and worth.

External Triggers:

External triggers stem from situations, environments, or interactions with others. These can range from crowded spaces and loud noises to conflictual relationships and high-pressure work environments. For instance, you may feel anxious and overwhelmed in social gatherings, especially if you sense tension or negativity in the atmosphere.

Consider the following scenarios illustrating internal and external triggers commonly encountered by highly sensitive women:

Internal Trigger Example:

You constantly berate yourself for not meeting your own high standards. This inner critic stems from childhood experiences of feeling like you never quite fit in or met the expectations of others. Whenever you make a mistake or fall short of your goals, you experience intense feelings of self-loathing and inadequacy.

External Trigger Example:

Working in a fast-paced office environment, you find yourself becoming increasingly stressed and overwhelmed by the constant noise and chaos around you. The loud conversations, ringing phones, and fluorescent lighting trigger sensory overload, leaving you feeling drained and anxious.

Exploring personal triggers is a journey of self-discovery and self-awareness for you as a highly sensitive woman.

The following prompts and exercises can aid in this process:

1. Journaling:

Keep a journal where you can express your thoughts, feelings, and experiences. Reflect on moments when you felt particularly overwhelmed, anxious, or upset. Explore the underlying triggers behind these emotions, noting any recurring patterns or themes.

Prompt: Reflect on a recent situation that left you feeling overwhelmed or anxious. Describe the event, your emotional reaction, and any thoughts or beliefs that may have contributed to your response.

2. Sensory Awareness Practices:

Engage in sensory awareness exercises to tune into your surroundings and internal sensations. Notice how different environments, sounds, textures, and smells impact your mood and energy levels. This heightened awareness can help you identify sensory triggers more effectively.

3. Self-Compassion Exercises:

Practice self-compassion and kindness towards yourself. Challenge self-critical thoughts and beliefs with affirmations and self-care practices. Remind yourself that it's okay to feel overwhelmed at times and that you deserve gentleness and understanding.

Positive Affirmation: "I am worthy of love and acceptance just as I am. I embrace my sensitivity as a beautiful aspect of who I am."

4. Boundary Setting:

Establish healthy boundaries in your relationships and environments. Identify situations or interactions that drain your energy or trigger negative emotions and explore ways to assert your needs and limits assertively.

Approach trigger identification with compassion and non-judgment. You may struggle with feelings of guilt or shame about your sensitivity or perceived weaknesses. However, understanding triggers is not about fault or blame but rather about fostering self-awareness and empowerment.

By cultivating non-judgmental awareness, you can:

- Create a safe space for self-exploration and growth.

- Develop resilience and adaptive coping strategies for managing triggers effectively.

- Cultivate self-acceptance and compassion towards your sensitive nature.

- Strengthen your emotional well-being and overall quality of life.

THE SCIENCE BEHIND YOUR EMOTIONS

Emotions are a fundamental aspect of human experience, influencing our thoughts, behaviors, and interactions with the world around us. Understanding the neurobiology of emotions provides valuable insight into how our brains process and respond to emotional stimuli. For highly sensitive women (HSWs), who possess a heightened sensitivity to stimuli and emotions, delving into the science behind emotions can offer a deeper understanding of their unique emotional experiences and empower them to manage their emotions effectively.

Emotions are complex, multifaceted experiences that involve various brain regions and neural pathways. At the core of emotional processing is the limbic system, a network of brain structures responsible for regulating emotions and memory. Key components of the limbic system include the amygdala, hippocampus, and prefrontal cortex.

The Amygdala: The Emotional Center

The amygdala plays a central role in the processing and regulation of emotions, particularly fear and anxiety. It receives sensory input from the environment and assesses the emotional significance of stimuli, triggering the appropriate emotional response. For example, when faced with a perceived threat, the amygdala initiates the body's stress response, activating the release of stress hormones like cortisol and adrenaline.

Sensitivity to Stimuli

HSWs often exhibit heightened sensitivity to sensory stimuli, including sights, sounds, smells, and social cues. This heightened sensory processing is thought to result from differences in neural connectivity and neurotransmitter activity within the brain. Research suggests that HSWs may have increased activation in regions of the brain associated with sensory processing, such as the sensory cortex and thalamus.

The amygdala's role in emotional processing is particularly relevant for HSWs, as they may exhibit heightened amygdala reactivity to emotional stimuli. This increased sensitivity can lead to more intense emotional responses and greater vulnerability to stress and anxiety. Additionally, HSWs may have differences in the connectivity between the amygdala and other brain regions involved in emotional regulation, such as the prefrontal cortex.

While research on the neurobiology of highly sensitive individuals is still emerging, studies have begun to uncover potential differences in brain structure and function. For example, neuroimaging studies have revealed differences in the volume and activity of brain regions involved in emotional processing, such as the amygdala and insula, in HSWs compared to non-sensitive individuals.

CULTIVATING SELF-AWARENESS: THE KEY TO EMOTIONAL REGULATION

Self-awareness is a cornerstone of emotional intelligence, essential for individuals to recognize and understand their own thoughts, feelings, and behaviors. For highly sensitive women (HSWs), who often experience emotions more intensely and deeply than others, self-awareness plays a critical role in emotional regulation and overall well-being.

Self-awareness involves introspection and self-reflection, enabling individuals to gain insight into their emotions, triggers, and coping mechanisms. For HSWs, who may be more prone to overwhelm due to their heightened sensitivity to stimuli, self-awareness is vital for managing emotions effectively and maintaining mental and emotional balance. It allows HSWs to recognize when they are becoming emotionally dysregulated and empowers them to implement coping strategies to regain equilibrium.

Emotional regulation is the ability to manage and respond to emotions in a healthy and adaptive manner. HSWs often face challenges related to managing intense emotions, navigating interpersonal dynamics, and setting boundaries in their personal and professional lives. Self-awareness provides HSWs with the foundation necessary to identify their emotional triggers, understand how they react to different stimuli, and develop strategies to regulate their emotions constructively.

Mindfulness practices offer powerful tools for enhancing self-awareness among HSWs, enabling them to cultivate present-moment awareness and observe their thoughts and emotions without judgment. These practices promote a deeper understanding of one's inner experiences and facilitate greater emotional resilience. Some mindfulness techniques that HSWs can integrate into their daily lives include:

1. Meditation: Regular meditation practice can help HSWs cultivate a sense of calm and clarity amidst the busyness of daily life. By dedicating time each day to sit quietly, focus on their breath, and observe their thoughts and feelings without getting caught up in them, HSWs can strengthen their self-awareness and emotional regulation skills.

2. Journaling: Writing can be a therapeutic tool for self-reflection and introspection. HSWs can maintain a journal to explore their thoughts, feelings, and experiences, allowing them to gain insights into their emotional patterns and triggers. Reflecting on journal entries can help HSWs identify areas for growth and develop strategies to manage their emotions more effectively.

3. Body Awareness Practices: Body awareness practices, such as body scans and progressive muscle relaxation, can help HSWs connect with their physical sensations and gain insight into how their bodies respond to stress and tension. By tuning into their bodies and observing any areas of discomfort or tension without judgment, HSWs can learn to release physical and emotional tension and promote relaxation.

Central to self-awareness is the ability to observe one's thoughts, feelings, and physical sensations with curiosity and acceptance, rather than judgment or resistance. HSWs can cultivate this skill by practicing self-compassion and adopting a non-judgmental stance towards their inner experiences. When faced with challenging emotions or intrusive thoughts, HSWs can employ the following techniques:

1. Mindful Awareness: Instead of reacting impulsively to emotions, HSWs can practice mindful awareness by pausing and observing their thoughts and feelings without immediately reacting to them. By creating space between stimulus and response, HSWs can choose how they want to respond to challenging situations and emotions.

2. Self-Compassion: HSWs can cultivate self-compassion by treating themselves with kindness and understanding, especially during times of emotional distress. By acknowledging their own humanity and inherent worth, HSWs can offer themselves the same level of compassion and care that they would offer to a close friend or loved one.

3. ***Non-Identification:*** HSWs can practice non-identification by recognizing that their thoughts and emotions are transient and impermanent. By viewing their thoughts and feelings as passing mental events rather than fixed aspects of their identity, HSWs can prevent themselves from becoming overwhelmed by challenging emotions and maintain a sense of perspective.

Proactively recognizing early warning signs of negative emotions allows HSWs to intervene before they escalate, enabling them to manage their emotions more effectively and prevent burnout. Some tips for recognizing these signs include:

1. ***Physical Cues:*** Pay attention to physical signs of stress or tension, such as muscle tension, headaches, or changes in appetite or sleep patterns. These physical cues can indicate underlying emotional distress that requires attention and self-care.

2. *Cognitive Patterns:* Notice repetitive or intrusive thoughts that contribute to negative emotions, such as self-doubt, perfectionism, or catastrophizing.

3. *Behavioral Changes:* Be mindful of changes in behavior, such as increased irritability, withdrawal from social interactions, or difficulty concentrating. These behavioral cues may indicate that HSWs are experiencing emotional distress and need to take steps to prioritize self-care and emotional regulation.

JOURNEYING THROUGH THE RAPIDS OF EMOTION

I paddle. Well, I own a couple of kayaks. Living out in the heart of scorching Texas, there's not much else to do but glide along the river's gentle flow. Now, I'd like to believe I'm a skilled kayaker. I confidently maneuver the waters, directing my fellow paddlers with assurance. Yet, despite my best efforts, the current often carries us off course. We find ourselves careening towards the shore or zigzagging aimlessly, expending unnecessary energy.

Picture this: the river as a metaphor for emotional regulation. On one bank lies a tumultuous cascade of fury, tears, and turmoil – the realm of explosive outbursts and unchecked emotions. On the opposite bank, a desolate stretch devoid of feeling, where emotions are suppressed and ignored, an icy expanse of detachment.

Trauma acts as a powerful force, accelerating the river's pace and drawing the banks closer together. It's no wonder we collide with them. Whether it's the loss of a loved one, the sting of abuse, or the upheaval of relocation, these experiences narrow our emotional channel, limiting our capacity to navigate the daily ebb and flow of feelings.

And that's alright.

If you find yourself easily provoked, teetering on the edge of emotional abyss, or retreating into numbness, remember: you're fragile. You're not alone in your struggle. Each narrow passage in our lives presents an opportunity to reconnect, to seek solace in faith, to ask for help, to extend grace to ourselves and others.

If you're fortunate to find yourself in a wider stretch of the river, where emotions flow steadily and serenely, don't grow complacent. Don't judge those still grappling with the rapids. Life's currents are unpredictable, and storms may lurk around the bend. Embrace this season of tranquility, but remain empathetic to those navigating rougher waters.

One of my children has weathered their fair share of storms. What some may misinterpret as behavioral issues are, in truth, the manifestations of past trauma, the struggle to process overwhelming emotions. They need our patience, our understanding, our unwavering support as they learn to navigate life's obstacles without crashing into the riverbank. And as we offer them grace, their emotional horizon expands.

Our rivers can widen. With the right support systems in place – safe spaces for reflection, professional guidance when needed – our capacity to regulate our emotions grows, allowing us to navigate the currents of life with greater ease and resilience.

CHAPTER 3

DECIPHERING THE

MESSAGES

Think of emotions like a big puzzle. Lots of things fit together to make them happen. Research says that our feelings can rub off on each other. It's like when someone smiles at you, you might feel like smiling back. Our outside feelings can affect how we feel inside, too. For example, if you smile, you might actually start feeling happier.

Other stuff can also change how we feel:

1. Physical Health: Sometimes, when our bodies aren't working right, our emotions can go a bit wonky too. Things like thyroid problems or diseases like Alzheimer's or Parkinson's can mess with how we feel. It's like they shake up our emotional world.

2. Genes: Our genes are like a set of instructions for our emotions. They help decide how we act and feel. Even though we can't change our genes, we can still do things to help our brains work better. With practice and trying new things, we can make our emotions more like how we want them to be.

3. Culture: Different groups of people have different rules about showing feelings. Some cultures think it's rude to express emotions in certain ways. So, what's okay in one place might not be okay somewhere else. It's like each culture has its own rulebook for emotions.

So, our feelings aren't just about what happens inside us. They're also influenced by the world around us, like our bodies, our genes, and the culture we're part of.

THE INTERPLAY OF THOUGHTS AND EMOTIONS

Emotions and thoughts, like dance partners, sway and twirl in a delicate choreography, each influencing the other in a symphony of internal dialogue. It's a dynamic relationship where our thoughts can kickstart an emotion or help us understand what we're feeling. Let's break it down with a couple of examples.

Imagine you have a big job interview coming up, and you start feeling nervous. You can tell yourself that this fear might not be entirely realistic. This kind of self-talk can help you see the situation from a different perspective, easing your emotional burden.

How we see and react to the world around us can also shape our feelings. Let's say you're afraid of dogs. Whenever you see one, you become hyper-aware, watching their every move. This heightened vigilance can trigger feelings of threat and distress. But someone else might see the same dog and view it as friendly, leading to a completely different emotional response.

But can we change our thoughts and emotions? Absolutely! Research tells us that our emotions aren't set in stone. Here are a few ways we can reshape them:

1. Change the Situation: Sometimes, altering our environment can change how we feel. For instance, leaving a toxic relationship can lift a heavy emotional burden.

2. Shift Your Focus: Decide to look at the brighter side of things. By focusing on the positive aspects of a situation, you can change how you feel about it.

3. Reframe the Situation: Instead of seeing a challenge as a threat, view it as an opportunity for growth. For example, think of a test as a chance to learn, not just a measure of your worth.

How we choose to live our lives has a huge impact on our emotions. Practices like positive thinking or mindfulness can help us see the world in a brighter light, making us feel happier and more resilient. And studies have shown that attitudes like kindness, gratitude, and forgiveness can be nurtured and cultivated over time.

Now, let's talk about defense mechanisms. These are like shields we use to protect ourselves from unpleasant thoughts or feelings. They're natural, but sometimes they can get in the way of dealing with our emotions effectively.

Denial is the most common defense mechanism. It's when we refuse to accept reality, blocking out painful events or feelings. You've probably heard people say, "They're in denial," when someone's ignoring the obvious.

Another common one is ***intellectualization***. This is when we focus on facts and logic to avoid dealing with emotions. For example, someone might lose their job and spend all their time making spreadsheets instead of facing their feelings.

Compartmentalization: Ever felt like your life is divided into separate boxes? That's compartmentalization. It's when you keep different parts of your life separate, like not bringing personal issues into the workplace. It's a way to protect yourself from challenges or anxieties in specific situations.

Reaction Formation: Sometimes, we feel one way but act the opposite. For example, someone might feel angry but respond with exaggerated cheerfulness. It's like wearing a mask to hide our true feelings.

Sublimation or Redirection: This one's a positive spin on defense mechanisms. Instead of letting strong emotions overwhelm us, we channel them into safe and constructive activities. For instance, turning frustration into a workout session or creative outlet.

Rationalization: Ever tried to justify a bad decision with "facts"? That's rationalization. It's a way to make ourselves feel better about choices we know aren't quite right. Like telling yourself you weren't interested in someone after they reject you.

Regression: When faced with anxiety or stress, some of us retreat into the past, behaving as we did when we were younger. Children might revert to thumb-sucking or bed-wetting after experiencing trauma. Adults might engage in childish behaviors like sleeping with stuffed animals or overeating comfort foods.

Displacement: Instead of lashing out at the source of our frustration, we redirect our anger towards something or someone less threatening. Like snapping at a loved one after a rough day at work.

Projection: Ever felt uncomfortable with your own thoughts or feelings, so you attribute them to someone else? That's projection. It's a way of deflecting our insecurities onto others. For instance, a bully projecting their own vulnerability onto a weaker target.

Repression: This one's about burying unpleasant memories or thoughts deep within our minds, hoping they'll disappear. Spoiler alert: they don't. They can still affect our behaviors and relationships, even if we pretend they're not there.

These defense mechanisms are like invisible guardians, shielding us from the storms of our inner worlds.

MASTERING YOUR EMOTIONS LIKE A BOSS

Emotions are like the colorful palette of our inner world, painting our experiences with vibrant hues of joy, sadness, anger, and everything in between. Being in tune with our emotions can be incredibly empowering, offering valuable insights that guide us through life's twists and turns. But when emotions run amok, they can wreak havoc on our relationships and well-being. Here's how you can take charge and become the boss of your emotions:

1. *Recognize the Time and Place*: Just like there's a time for laughter and a time for tears, there's a right time and place for intense emotions. While it's natural to grieve when we lose someone dear or to feel anger when we're wronged, it's crucial to exercise restraint in certain situations. Yelling at your boss won't solve anything. Being mindful of the context helps you decide whether it's okay to express your feelings or if it's better to take a moment to reflect.

2. *Take a Deep Breath:* Ah, the power of breath! In moments of intense emotion, slow down and pay attention to your breathing. Deep breathing exercises can be a lifeline, helping you regain control and find your center amidst the storm. Inhale deeply, feeling the breath fill your belly, hold for a moment, and then exhale slowly. Repeat a calming mantra to yourself, like "I am relaxed" or "I am calm."

3. *Create Space:* Sometimes, a little distance can work wonders. Physically removing yourself from a stressful situation or mentally distracting yourself can give you the clarity you need to respond thoughtfully. Remember, it's okay to take a break from your feelings temporarily, but don't forget to come back to them when you're ready. Spend time with your furry friend, confide in a trusted friend, or indulge in a good laugh.

4. *Tackle Stress Head-On:* Stress can be the kryptonite to our emotional superpowers. Finding healthy ways to manage stress is key to keeping our emotions in check. Whether it's through hobbies, relaxation techniques, or spending time in nature, make self-care a priority. Exercise, laughter, and quality sleep are your allies in the battle against stress.

5. *Embrace Meditation:* If you're already familiar with meditation, you're one step ahead. Meditation isn't just about finding inner peace; it's about embracing all facets of your experience, including your emotions. Through meditation, you learn to sit with your feelings without judgment or the need to change them. Acceptance is the first step towards regulation. Plus, meditation offers additional benefits like improved sleep and relaxation.

Harnessing the Power of Journaling

Keeping a journal can be your secret weapon in the battle against unruly emotions. By putting pen to paper, you unlock a world of self-discovery and reflection, paving the way for greater emotional awareness and control. Here's how to make the most of your journaling practice:

1. *Trace Patterns:* One of the primary benefits of journaling is its ability to help you identify patterns in your emotional responses. By writing about your feelings and the events that trigger them, you can gain valuable insights into the recurring themes or circumstances that contribute to difficult emotions. For example, you may notice that certain situations at work always leave you feeling stressed or anxious. By pinpointing these triggers, you can develop strategies to manage them more effectively, ultimately leading to greater emotional stability.

2. *Daily Reflection:* Consistency is key when it comes to journaling. Make it a daily habit to jot down your thoughts and feelings, particularly during moments of heightened emotion. Keeping your journal handy allows you to capture intense emotions in real-time, providing you with a record of your emotional experiences over time. Reviewing these entries can offer valuable insights into your emotional patterns and help you track your progress in managing difficult emotions.

3. Acceptance: A fundamental aspect of emotional regulation is learning to accept your feelings without judgment or resistance. Avoid downplaying your emotions or telling yourself to "just calm down." Instead, view your emotions as messengers, delivering important information about your inner world. Embracing them allows you to acknowledge and validate your experiences, fostering a sense of self-compassion and understanding.

4. Identify Your Feelings: When faced with intense emotions, take a moment to check in with yourself and identify what you're feeling. Ask yourself questions such as "What am I feeling right now?" and "What caused these feelings?" This process of introspection can help you gain clarity about the root causes of your emotions and better understand your emotional responses. By acknowledging and labeling your feelings, you empower yourself to navigate them more effectively.

5. Practice, Practice, Practice: Like any skill, emotional regulation requires practice and repetition. Challenge yourself to incorporate journaling into your daily routine and actively engage with the process of self-reflection. Experiment with different writing prompts and techniques to find what works best for you. Over time, you'll develop greater emotional resilience and a deeper understanding of yourself.

Embrace Regulation, Not Repression

Imagine if your emotions had a volume knob. You wouldn't want them blasting at max all day or completely muted. Similarly, repressing or suppressing emotions, whether consciously or unconsciously, hinders expression and experience, potentially leading to various health issues:

- Substance abuse

- Stress management difficulties

- Pain and muscle tension

- Sleep problems

- Depression

- Anxiety

When learning to manage emotions, avoid sweeping them under the rug. Healthy emotional expression strikes a balance between numbness and overwhelm.

Acknowledge Emotional Impact

Intense emotions enrich life, indicating full engagement rather than stifling natural reactions. Occasional overwhelm is normal, triggered by both joyous and distressing events.

Consistently out-of-control emotions may lead to:

- Emotional or physical outbursts

- Substance abuse

- Academic or occupational issues

- Social difficulties

- Interpersonal conflicts

Reflect on how emotions influence daily life to pinpoint problematic areas.

CHAPTER 4

SHIFTING YOUR MINDSET

Have you ever pondered why some individuals seem to effortlessly excel in various circumstances while others struggle to shine, despite possessing evident talents? Delving into research sheds light on the critical role of mindset in shaping our abilities and outcomes.

Consider the remarkable journeys of those who have achieved greatness. Many of them encountered naysayers who doubted their potential. Despite facing discouragement, they remained steadfast in their belief in themselves and diligently pursued their goals through hard work and perseverance.

Understanding Fixed vs. Growth Mindset

Central to the discussion of mindset are two distinct perspectives:

1. Fixed Mindset: This mindset suggests that our abilities and skills are predetermined and unchangeable. According to this belief, individuals are born with a set level of talent, and no amount of effort or practice can alter it.

2. Growth Mindset: In contrast, the growth mindset posits that abilities can be developed and improved over

time through dedication, hard work, and resilience. Those who subscribe to this mindset view challenges as opportunities for growth and believe that anyone can enhance their skills through effort and persistence.

While the advantages of cultivating a growth mindset may seem self-evident, it's essential to recognize that many individuals still cling to fixed mindsets in various aspects of their lives. Unfortunately, this rigid mindset can hinder personal and professional growth by limiting one's willingness to embrace challenges and pursue opportunities for development.

The beliefs we hold about our abilities profoundly influence our behavior and, consequently, our outcomes. Research indicates that students who embrace a growth mindset tend to experience improvement in their academic performance over time. Conversely, those who subscribe to a fixed mindset may find themselves stuck in a cycle of underachievement, as they perceive their intelligence as fixed and immutable.

Empowering Beliefs Lead to Success

At the heart of the matter lies the empowering belief that we have control over our abilities and destinies. While persistence, effort, and hard work undoubtedly play vital roles in achieving success, it is our belief in our capacity for growth and improvement that ultimately propels us forward.

Neuroscientific studies offer fascinating insights into how mindset influences our brain activity. Individuals with fixed mindsets tend to focus on external outcomes and judgments, while those with growth mindsets are more attuned to opportunities for learning and development.

The shift from a fixed mindset to a growth mindset entails a fundamental change in perspective. Rather than fixating on outcomes and judgments, individuals with a growth mindset prioritize learning, development, and continuous improvement. It is this mindset that lays the foundation for a brighter and more fulfilling future. So, instead of asking, "How did I do?" adopt the mindset of asking, "What can I do better next time?" This simple shift in mindset can unlock your full potential and pave the way for success in all aspects of life.

Mindsets significantly influence how individuals respond to setbacks. Those with a growth mindset perceive setbacks as opportunities for learning and growth, motivating them to redouble their efforts in overcoming challenges. On the contrary, individuals with a fixed mindset often feel discouraged by setbacks, viewing them as evidence of their limitations. Consequently, they may lose interest and give up on their endeavors.

Contrary to the notion that "old dogs can't learn new tricks," the human brain possesses remarkable plasticity. Neuroplasticity, as neuroscientists call it, refers to the brain's ability to adapt and rewire itself throughout life. This phenomenon contradicts earlier beliefs that brain plasticity was limited to childhood, as research now demonstrates that the brain remains malleable even in adulthood.

Neural plasticity occurs through the formation of new pathways in the brain, which are established through repeated thoughts and actions. Over time, these pathways become ingrained as habits, shaping our behaviors and thought patterns. Recognizing the potential for change, individuals can actively reshape their internal programming by consciously engaging in new experiences and learning opportunities.

Cultivating a growth mindset involves a deliberate commitment to personal growth and development. By embracing the science-backed concept of growth mindset, individuals can not only enhance their own abilities but also empower others to adopt a similar perspective. Recognizing one's capacity for growth instills a sense of control over one's life, leading to improved performance and resilience in the face of challenges.

Internalize the principles of a growth mindset by challenging the critical voice of your fixed mindset. Whenever self-doubt creeps in, remind yourself that you have the capacity to learn and grow, dismissing negative thoughts that undermine your potential.

A growth mindset transcends mere academic or professional pursuits; it permeates every aspect of life. Whether at work, in relationships, or in sports, adopting a growth mindset fosters a proactive approach to learning and improvement, enhancing overall well-being and success.

Creating a growth mindset is not merely advantageous; it's essential for achieving one's aspirations in life. By recognizing the potential for growth and improvement, individuals can break free from self-imposed limitations and strive for greater fulfillment and success.

The notion of innate intelligence is a complex one. While genetic factors may initially influence aptitude, individuals with a growth mindset believe in the power of effort and persistence to surpass inherent talents. Teachers play a crucial role in fostering this outlook by providing continuous feedback and encouragement, unlocking students' potential for growth and development.

Humans possess the capacity for both growth and fixed mindsets, depending on the context. While fixed mindsets may be appropriate in certain situations, such as recognizing limitations like inability to fly, a growth mindset fosters a mindset of continuous improvement and resilience.

Have you ever considered whether your abilities and skills are fixed from birth, or if they can evolve and develop over time? Reflect on your beliefs regarding the following statements:

1. "It's hard for me to lose weight."

2. "I'm not good with numbers."

3. "I'm not an athlete."

4. "I'm not creative."

5. "I'm a procrastinator."

If you find yourself agreeing with these statements, it's likely you hold a fixed mindset. This mindset tends to avoid situations where failure is a possibility.

On the other hand, if you believe that your beliefs and capabilities can evolve, and that intelligence and wisdom can expand through new experiences, you likely possess a growth mindset.

It's important to note that it's okay if you currently have a fixed mindset. You have the power to cultivate a growth mindset, and we'll explore how to do so below.

Why Does It Matter?

Our approach to learning and challenges can significantly impact our attitude and outcomes. A positive mindset can mean the difference between giving up when faced with difficulty and persevering through challenges, ultimately leading to personal growth.

A growth mindset isn't solely about effort; it's about valuing the process over the outcome. While those with a fixed mindset may see failure as wasted effort, individuals with a growth mindset appreciate every step of the journey, regardless of the result. They tackle challenges head-on, continuously seeking opportunities for growth and improvement.

Overcoming Fixed Mindset Limitations

Having a fixed mindset may lead one to shy away from challenges to avoid potential humiliation or embarrassment. However, avoiding challenges can hinder personal growth and prevent individuals from realizing their full potential.

In contrast, those with a growth mindset embrace challenges as opportunities for learning and growth. They prioritize personal development over the fear of failure, recognizing that stepping outside of their comfort zone is essential for progress.

Individuals with a growth mindset thrive on facing challenges, as they view them as opportunities for growth and learning. While they may not always have all the answers, their willingness to try new things and persevere through difficulties enables them to develop new skills and broaden their life experiences.

Cultivating a growth mindset can lead to a richer, more fulfilling life, characterized by continuous growth and learning.

WAYS TO CULTIVATE YOUR GROWTH MINDSET

Transitioning from a fixed mindset to a growth mindset may initially appear daunting, yet it's an achievable endeavor through consistent effort and determination. Embracing imperfections is the first step toward cultivating a growth mindset. By acknowledging and celebrating both our own and others' flaws and unique qualities, we create a foundation for self-acceptance and growth. Challenges, often perceived as daunting obstacles, can be reframed as opportunities for personal development and exploration. Instead of succumbing to fear or doubt, viewing challenges as avenues for growth fosters resilience and a willingness to engage in new experiences.

Monitoring our internal dialogue and language usage is crucial in fostering a growth mindset. By replacing negative self-talk with positive affirmations and embracing a mindset of acceptance, compassion, and confidence, we pave the way for personal growth. Seeking validation from within rather than external sources is another pivotal aspect of developing a growth mindset. Trusting our own judgment and capabilities empowers us to navigate challenges with self-assurance and determination.

Authenticity serves as a guiding principle in the journey toward a growth mindset. Embracing our true selves and avoiding pretense allows us to align our actions with our values and aspirations authentically. Discovering our sense of purpose is a transformative step in cultivating a growth mindset. Through introspection and reflection, we uncover our passions and motivations, propelling us toward meaningful endeavors with clarity and purpose.

Recognizing and appreciating our unique strengths while actively working to improve areas of weakness is essential for nurturing a growth mindset. Constructive criticism, viewed as an opportunity for learning and growth rather than a personal attack, provides valuable insights for improvement. Valuing the process over results encourages a mindset of continuous learning and development, emphasizing the importance of the journey toward achieving our goals.

Embracing a "not yet" mentality reframes setbacks as temporary obstacles on the path to mastery, fostering perseverance and resilience. Taking risks and embracing vulnerability allows us to step outside our comfort zones, facilitating personal growth and discovery. Setting realistic timelines and focusing on the effort and engagement invested in the process rather than fixating on speed cultivates patience and perseverance.

Ultimately, owning our attitude and actively working to cultivate a growth-oriented mindset is key. By embracing resilience and persistence, we unlock opportunities for growth and transformation, fostering a sense of empowerment and fulfillment in our journey toward personal and professional development.

CHAPTER 5

UNRAVELING THE DYNAMICS

OF NEGATIVITY

In our daily lives, negative thinking occasionally creeps in, but chronic negativity can wreak havoc on our mental well-being, leading to feelings of anxiety and depression. Scientific research highlights the profound impact of positive thinking on mental health, stress levels, and even cardiovascular health. However, many of us find ourselves ensnared in persistent negative thought patterns.

Distinguishing between ordinary worries and negative thinking can be challenging upon introspection. It's normal to experience moments of sadness or concern regarding various life challenges, such as relationship issues or financial burdens. However, when these emotions become pervasive and repetitive, they may signify deeper underlying issues. Negative thinking manifests as a pessimistic outlook on oneself and the surrounding environment. While occasional negative thoughts are common, persistent negativity that distorts one's perception of self and the world may indicate mental health concerns. It's essential to recognize that not everyone experiencing negative thinking will develop a mental illness, but chronic negative thoughts can significantly impair quality of life and mental well-being.

Understanding Negativity Bias

The tendency to focus more on negative events than positive ones, known as negativity bias, profoundly influences our perceptions and behaviors. Negative experiences tend to leave a more profound impact than positive ones, shaping our actions, decisions, and interpersonal relationships. Negativity bias manifests in various ways, including heightened sensitivity to negative stimuli, a tendency to recall negative events more vividly than positive ones, and a greater emotional response to criticism compared to praise. This bias explains why negative first impressions linger and past traumas continue to haunt us, overshadowing positive experiences.

Negativity bias influences not only our emotional responses but also our motivation and decision-making processes. Research indicates that individuals are often more motivated to avoid loss than to pursue gain, emphasizing the potent influence of negativity on goal-directed behavior. Moreover, negativity bias affects how we perceive information, leading us to assign greater validity to negative news due to its attention-grabbing nature.

Evolutionary Roots of Negativity Bias

This propensity towards negativity may have evolutionary roots, rooted in the survival imperative of early humans. In a world fraught with dangers, those who were more attuned to potential threats were more likely to survive and pass down their genes. Hence, our brains have evolved to prioritize processing negative stimuli, as they signal potential dangers and evoke survival instincts. Neuroscience corroborates this notion, demonstrating increased neural processing in response to negative stimuli, as evidenced by heightened cerebral cortex activity when exposed to negative images.

Negativity bias reflects our brain's adaptive response to the environment, shaped by millennia of evolutionary pressure. While negativity bias served as a survival mechanism in our ancestral past, its persistence in modern times underscores the importance of cultivating awareness and mindfulness to counteract its detrimental effects on mental well-being.

Understanding the root causes of negative thoughts is crucial for effectively managing and overcoming them. While intrusive negative thoughts can indicate underlying mental health conditions such as generalized anxiety disorder, OCD, or depression, they can also stem from common life stressors and internal programming. Exploring the primary causes of negative thoughts can shed light on strategies for mitigating their impact.

Fear of the Future

One significant cause of negative thinking is the fear of the unknown future. Many individuals grapple with uncertainty and apprehension about what lies ahead, leading to catastrophic thinking patterns. This tendency to envision the worst-case scenarios can drain one's energy and amplify feelings of anxiety. However, accepting the inherent unpredictability of the future and focusing on the present moment can help alleviate these negative thoughts. By cultivating mindfulness and embracing the present, you can reduce the grip of future-oriented worries on your mental well-being.

Anxiety about the Present

Anxiety about current circumstances is another common trigger for negative thinking. Concerns about interpersonal relationships, work performance, and daily hassles can fuel pessimistic thought patterns, leading individuals to anticipate unfavorable outcomes. Negative thinkers often envision exaggerated worst-case scenarios, such as believing that colleagues dislike them or anticipating reprimand from their boss. These distorted perceptions stem from a fear of losing control over one's life. Establishing routines, organizational strategies, and seeking support through therapy can provide practical avenues for managing present-oriented anxiety and alleviating negative thoughts.

Shame about the Past

Reflecting on past failures and mistakes often fuels feelings of shame and regret, contributing to persistent negative thinking. Many individuals find themselves ruminating over past disappointments, replaying scenarios in their minds and dwelling on perceived shortcomings. However, dwelling on past missteps serves little purpose beyond perpetuating negative thought patterns. Instead, adopting a constructive approach involves accepting past mistakes, learning from them, and focusing on strategies for personal growth and improvement. By reframing past experiences as opportunities for learning and growth, you can break free from the cycle of shame and self-criticism.

The inability to simply "stop" negative thoughts is a common struggle for individuals grappling with intrusive and persistent negativity. Hearing simplistic admonitions like "just be happy" can evoke feelings of hopelessness and frustration. Experiencing negative thoughts doesn't reflect one's character or morality; it's a complex interplay of psychological factors.

Negative thoughts often feel compelling and difficult to shake off because they trigger the brain's reward system, leading to the release of feel-good chemicals like dopamine. This neurochemical reward reinforces the recurrence of negative thoughts, turning them into habitual patterns. These habits become deeply ingrained within the basal ganglia, the primitive part of the brain sometimes referred to as the "lizard brain."

Due to their origin in this ancient region of the brain, these negative thought patterns become deeply entrenched, making them challenging to break. Some scientists even suggest that these habits cannot be eradicated but only replaced with new ones. For instance, someone accustomed to taking a smoke break to alleviate boredom may eventually replace that habit with chewing gum.

However, negative thoughts aren't merely habits; they can evolve into addictive patterns. When the brain perceives negativity as rewarding, it can become addicted to those thought patterns. Unfortunately, attempts to replace one addiction with another may lead to equally harmful behaviors like substance abuse.

Despite the seeming bleakness of this situation, there is hope for individuals struggling with negative thoughts.

IMPACT OF NEGATIVE THINKING

Transitioning from occasional negative thoughts to constant and intrusive negativity can pose significant dangers to both mental and physical health. Prolonged exposure to negative thought patterns can contribute to the development of mood disorders, such as depression and chronic anxiety, as well as exacerbate existing conditions like high blood pressure.

The impact of negativity isn't limited to mental health; it manifests physically in various ways, including drastic changes in metabolism, sleep disturbances, upset stomach, fatigue, chest pains, and headaches. Social withdrawal, depression, anxiety, and even severe mental health conditions like schizophrenia and personality disorders can stem from unchecked negative thoughts.

The detrimental effects of constant negativity stem from its role in chronic stress. Persistent stress disrupts hormonal balance, compromises the immune system, and depletes neurotransmitters crucial for emotional well-being. Ultimately, chronic stress can shorten lifespan and contribute to various health issues, including high blood pressure, infections, digestive disorders, and cardiovascular disease.

Cynicism, a common manifestation of negative thinking, has been linked to serious consequences. Research conducted by the American Academy of Neurology found that high levels of cynicism later in life correlate with a heightened risk of dementia, independent of other risk factors like smoking and heart health markers. This underscores the pervasive influence of negative thoughts on long-term health outcomes.

Moreover, negative emotions often trigger unhealthy coping mechanisms such as excessive drinking, smoking, or other harmful habits, further exacerbating the detrimental effects on overall well-being. The interconnectedness of our emotions, thoughts, and physical health underscores the importance of addressing negative thought patterns and cultivating strategies for promoting mental and physical resilience.

Negativity doesn't just affect individuals; it can significantly impact relationships, particularly romantic ones. The inherent negativity bias in human psychology means that individuals tend to focus more on their partner's faults rather than their strengths, leading to a magnification of perceived flaws and a minimization of positive attributes. This bias, coupled with a tendency to overestimate one's own virtues, can create a sense of resentment and unappreciation within the relationship.

Research conducted by psychologists on relationship satisfaction over time has revealed that while initial infatuation may fade, successful marriages are characterized by the ability to prevent a decline in satisfaction rather than constant improvement.

However, if the decline in satisfaction becomes steep, it can jeopardize the future of the relationship.

Consider a scenario where a partner does something that annoys the other. The response to such situations can be categorized into constructive and destructive strategies, each with active or passive manifestations. Constructive strategies involve addressing the issue openly and working towards a compromise, while destructive strategies include withdrawing silently or resorting to threats and ultimatums.

Interestingly, research suggests that while constructive strategies contribute positively to the relationship, they may not have a significant long-term impact. On the other hand, engaging in destructive behaviors, such as silent withdrawal or threats, can lead to a detrimental spiral of retaliation, placing immense strain on the relationship.

Negative thinking patterns can be challenging to identify because they often feel unquestionably true. However, recognizing and addressing these patterns is essential for promoting mental well-being. Here are three common negative thought patterns and strategies to transform them into healthier alternatives:

1. Negative Rumination:

Negative rumination involves getting mentally stuck and repeatedly dwelling on negative outcomes or experiences. While self-reflection can be healthy, excessive rumination can lead to increased anxiety and a sense of being stagnant. When you notice yourself ruminating, it's crucial to interrupt this pattern. Engage in activities that shift your focus away from negative thoughts, such as taking a walk or talking to a friend. However, be mindful not to discuss the content of your rumination during conversations to prevent reinforcing negative thinking.

2. Overthinking:

Overthinking occurs when you excessively analyze various options and potential outcomes, attempting to control uncontrollable future events. This pattern of thinking can lead to decision paralysis and heightened stress. To counter overthinking, set a deadline for making decisions and limit the time spent deliberating. Focus on researching a few alternative options rather than exhaustively considering every possibility. Embrace the uncertainty inherent in decision-making and trust in your ability to adapt to whatever outcome arises.

3. Cynical Hostility:

Cynical hostility involves viewing others with mistrust and interpreting their actions in the worst possible light. This negative thinking pattern can strain relationships and foster a pervasive sense of distrust. To combat cynical hostility, practice distancing yourself from judgmental thoughts and challenge negative interpretations of others' behavior. Consider alternative perspectives that may explain people's actions in a more positive or benign light. Strive to reserve judgment until you have sufficient evidence and reflect on how your own actions may influence interpersonal dynamics.

Overcoming negativity requires proactive strategies to address and transform negative thought patterns. Here are additional methods to help you manage and reduce negative thoughts effectively:

1. Schedule Your Negative Thoughts:

Paradoxically, setting aside a specific time each day, like ten minutes, to review and ruminate on negative thoughts can help you gain control over them. When negative thoughts arise throughout the day, write them down and save them for your designated "Negative Thought Time" (NTT). Limit this time to ten minutes daily, gradually gaining control over your negative thought patterns.

2. Replace Negative Thoughts:

Replacing negative thoughts with positive ones involves a four-step process. First, become aware of when negative thought patterns emerge. Acknowledge these patterns and express a desire to change them. Articulate alternative behaviors aligned with your goals, and consciously choose positive thoughts to replace the negative ones.

3. Write It Down:

Documenting the reasons behind your negative thoughts can facilitate their understanding and processing. Writing down negative thoughts helps externalize them, making it easier to gain insight and clarity. Seeing these thoughts on paper can aid in identifying patterns and developing strategies for managing them effectively.

4. Ask Tough Questions:

Reflect on challenging questions to gain deeper insight into your negative thought patterns. Consider the underlying motivations behind these thoughts and the potential benefits of adopting a more positive mindset. Explore past experiences that may have influenced your negativity and determine actionable steps to cultivate positivity in the present.

5. Limit Exposure to Negative News:

Research indicates that consuming negative news, particularly in the morning, can increase the likelihood of experiencing negative emotions throughout the day. Conversely, maintaining a positive mindset can enhance satisfaction and productivity. Consider reducing or eliminating exposure to negative news sources in the morning to promote a more optimistic outlook and improve overall well-being.

Incorporating these strategies into your daily routine can empower you to effectively manage negative thoughts and cultivate a more positive and resilient mindset.

CHAPTER 6

GRASPING ANGER

What is anger, exactly? It's one of our core emotions, just like feeling disgusted, anxious, sad, or happy. These emotions are essential for our survival, shaped by our history. Anger is closely linked to our instinctive responses: freeze, flee, or fight. It's the emotion that gears us up for a fight. But fighting doesn't always mean physical combat; it can also spur communities to confront injustice by changing laws or behaviors.

If you find yourself getting angry too often or too easily, it can damage your relationships and even harm your health. Experiencing frequent bursts of anger releases stress hormones that can harm the brain's neurons responsible for short-term memory and sound judgment. Moreover, it weakens the immune system.

We've all experienced that surge of rage when someone cuts us off in traffic. The urge to retaliate by flooring the gas pedal or making obscene gestures is strong. But expressing anger doesn't make it disappear; it can actually fuel and intensify it.

Like any other emotion, anger requires self-awareness to prevent it from escalating into violent, aggressive, or hostile actions towards others or oneself. Many cities offer support groups to help manage anger, either through individual or group sessions. Cognitive restructuring techniques can also be effective, as they help individuals reframe their inflammatory and unhealthy thoughts.

Anger is a natural emotion that everyone experiences at some point. However, it becomes problematic when its intensity or frequency starts interfering with mental health, legal standing, job performance, or relationships. While there isn't an official diagnosis for an "anger disorder," dysfunctional anger can be a symptom of conditions like manic episodes, intermittent explosive disorder, or borderline personality disorder. You don't need a formal diagnosis to recognize when anger becomes disruptive or to seek help in managing it.

THE ROOT CAUSE OF ANGER

Anger can stem from various sources, and recognizing these triggers is the first step in managing it effectively. Here are nine main reasons why anger may arise:

1. Unmet Needs or Threats to Safety

According to Maslow's hierarchy of needs, our basic requirements for survival and happiness must be fulfilled before higher-level needs can be addressed. When necessities like food, water, warmth, rest, security, and safety are lacking, anger can emerge as we're compelled to fight for these essentials. The longer these needs remain unmet, the more intense our drive to satisfy them becomes, ultimately affecting our overall well-being.

2. Grief and Loss

Experiencing the loss of a loved one can trigger anger as it threatens our fundamental human needs and disrupts various aspects of our lives. The changes that accompany loss, such as shifts in location, financial circumstances, and family dynamics, contribute to feelings of anger. This anger can manifest in different ways, including frustration towards the departed, resentment towards a higher power, or even anger towards the illness that caused the loss.

3. Violation of Boundaries

Healthy boundaries are essential for protecting ourselves from exploitation and maintaining our emotional well-being. When these boundaries are disregarded or violated by others, anger may arise as a response. It's often a sign that someone has been disregarding our boundaries for an extended period, disrespecting our feelings, and attempting to exert control over us.

4. Disappointment and Unrealized Expectations

Feeling disappointed or let down, whether by ourselves or others, can lead to anger, especially when our basic needs for security and reliability are involved. Disappointment often arises when things don't go as planned or when individuals fail to meet our expectations, particularly if they hold significant roles in our lives.

5. Guilt and Shame

Anger can serve as a defense mechanism to mask feelings of guilt and shame, especially in response to criticism or feedback. By reacting defensively and redirecting attention away from these painful emotions, individuals may resort to anger as a coping strategy.

6. Unforgiveness and Resentment

Bitterness, resentment, and the desire for revenge are all manifestations of unresolved anger triggered by perceived injustices or unfair treatment. Failure to forgive and let go of past grievances can escalate these emotions, leading to prolonged and intensified feelings of anger.

7. Vitamin Deficiency

Surprisingly, deficiencies in certain B vitamins, such as B1 and B5, can contribute to irritability and anger due to their role in maintaining brain health. A lack of these micronutrients in the diet can lead to imbalances that affect mood regulation.

8. Substance Abuse

Substance abuse often coexists with anger, as individuals may turn to drugs or alcohol in an attempt to numb or alleviate their intense emotions. However, substance use typically exacerbates feelings of anger, making them more difficult to manage in the long run.

9. Unresolved Childhood Trauma

Childhood experiences of unhealthy expression or suppression of anger can manifest in adulthood as unresolved emotional distress. Individuals who have learned to suppress their anger may struggle to cope with it effectively, leading to its buildup and eventual release in unhealthy ways.

Keeping your anger in check is crucial to prevent saying or doing things you might regret later. Here are some strategies to help you control your anger before it spirals out of control:

1. Channel Your Creativity

Transform your anger into a creative outlet. Consider writing poetry, tending to your garden, or painting when you feel upset. Emotions can serve as inspiration for creative endeavors, providing a constructive way to alleviate anger.

2. Express Yourself

It's healthy to express your emotions, as long as it's done in a constructive manner. Confide in a trusted friend who can hold you accountable. Engaging in mature conversations can help alleviate anger and prevent future conflicts.

3. Practice Empathy

Put yourself in someone else's shoes and try to see the situation from their perspective. Understanding their point of view may lead to a better comprehension of the situation and reduce your anger.

4. Write It Out

Draft an email or letter expressing your feelings to the person who angered you, but refrain from sending it. Simply writing down your emotions can be cathartic, even if the message remains unsent.

5. Find Humor

Laughter can dispel a bad mood effectively. Engage in activities that make you laugh, whether it's scrolling through memes, watching comedy shows, or spending time with loved ones.

6. Change Your Routine

Modify your daily routine to avoid triggers that provoke anger. If your commute to work fuels your frustration, explore alternative routes that may take longer but spare you unnecessary stress.

7. Pause and Reflect

Before reacting impulsively, take a moment to pause and consider your response to the situation. Reflecting on various solutions can prevent outbursts and help you respond more calmly.

8. Seek Immediate Solutions

Identify quick fixes to alleviate your anger in the moment. For instance, if your child's messy room frustrates you, simply close the door to temporarily remove the source of irritation.

9. Journal Your Thoughts

Write down your feelings and thoughts in a journal as an outlet for emotions you can't express directly to others. Processing your emotions through writing can promote self-reflection and emotional regulation.

10. Take Action

Redirect your anger into productive activities, such as advocating for change or performing acts of kindness. Channeling your energy into constructive endeavors can foster a sense of empowerment and alleviate anger.

11. Give Yourself a Timeout

Take a break from the situation and spend some quiet time alone. Use this opportunity to process your emotions and restore your inner calm. Regular timeouts can become a valuable part of your self-care routine.

12. Listen to Music

Music has a calming effect on the mind and soul. Escape into your favorite tunes to distract yourself from negative emotions and uplift your mood.

13. Mentally Escape

Find a peaceful mental retreat by visualizing yourself in a serene environment, such as a tranquil beach or lush forest. Immerse yourself in the details of this imaginary place to find solace amidst anger.

14. Go for a Walk

Engage in physical activity like walking, cycling, or working out to release pent-up anger and reduce stress levels. Exercise stimulates endorphin production, promoting a sense of well-being and tranquility.

15. Count

Use counting as a mindfulness technique to calm your anger. Whether counting up or down in increments of ten, focusing on numbers can help regulate your breathing and heart rate, dissipating anger gradually.

Ignoring or suppressing your emotions, whether it's frustration, grief, sadness, or anger, can have both short-term and long-term consequences on your physical and mental well-being. When emotions are suppressed, it creates internal stress on the body, regardless of the specific emotion being suppressed. This prolonged suppression can negatively impact various aspects of health, including self-esteem, memory, and blood pressure. Long-term suppression of emotions has been linked to an increased risk of heart disease and diabetes, as well as mental health issues such as depression, anxiety, aggression, and memory problems.

Moreover, suppressing emotions doesn't make them disappear; instead, it often amplifies them over time. For instance, if you're angry at someone but choose not to address it, the anger may intensify and eventually manifest in an outburst or explosion of emotions in unrelated situations, like experiencing road rage over a minor traffic incident. This buildup of suppressed emotions can lead to uncontrollable outbursts and heightened emotional reactions.

Managing intense emotions can be challenging, but there are strategies to help you cope:

1. Take Time for Self-Care:

Engage in activities that promote relaxation and well-being, such as meditation, aerobic exercise, or practicing gratitude and forgiveness. Taking care of your physical and mental health can help regulate emotions and reduce stress.

2. Own Your Response:

Reflect on how you've reacted to situations in the past and consider ways to respond differently in the future. Identify triggers and develop coping mechanisms to prevent emotional escalation. For unavoidable situations like grief, explore coping strategies to navigate through difficult emotions effectively.

3. Confront the Issue:

If possible, address the situation or person causing your emotional distress with the intention of resolving the problem constructively. If direct confrontation isn't feasible, practice "observing" the situation objectively, detaching yourself from personal biases and emotions. This perspective allows for a deeper understanding of others' motivations and behaviors, reducing feelings of frustration or anger.

4. Acknowledge Your Emotions:

Recognize and validate your feelings, even if they're complex or uncomfortable. Take time to identify the underlying emotions behind your reactions and ask yourself probing questions to understand your emotional responses better. This self-awareness can lead to healthier emotional processing and management.

CONCLUSION

Dear wonderful souls,

As you navigate this intricate journey of life, remember that your sensitivity is not a weakness, but a beautiful strength. Your ability to feel deeply, to empathize profoundly, and to see the world through a kaleidoscope of emotions is a gift beyond measure.

In moments of doubt or overwhelm, know that you are not alone. Your sensitivity binds you to a tribe of kindred spirits who understand and embrace the depth of your being. Embrace your vulnerability as a badge of honor, for it is a testament to your courage in a world that often demands toughness.

Take solace in the knowledge that your sensitivity is a superpower, allowing you to connect with others on a profound level and to bring light to the darkest of places. Embrace self-care rituals that nourish your spirit, surround yourself with people who honor your sensitivity, and never forget the power of your own inner resilience.

Above all, remember to be gentle with yourself. You are doing the best you can with the tools you have, and that is more than enough. Trust in your journey, honor your truth, and know that your sensitivity is a beacon of love and compassion in a world that sorely needs it.

If you've found solace, guidance, or inspiration within the pages of our shared journey, I kindly invite you to consider leaving a positive review and a heartfelt rating for the book on Amazon. Your words have the power to uplift others who may be seeking the same comfort and understanding that you've discovered.

By sharing your experience, you not only honor the work that has gone into creating this book but also contribute to a ripple effect of positivity and empowerment within our community of sensitive souls. Your voice matters, and your feedback can make a meaningful difference in someone else's life.

Thank you for considering this small gesture of support. Together, let's continue to spread compassion, empathy, and encouragement to all who walk this path beside us.

With heartfelt gratitude,

-SANDY MATHIAS

www.ingramcontent.com/pod-product-compliance
Lightning Source LLC
Chambersburg PA
CBHW050831260726
48660CB00006B/2170